Within My Window

(A collection of "thoughts-full" poetry)

ISBN No. 978-0-6152-0371-3

(Original copyright of many poems were in 1996, 1997, and 1998, as noted.)

BriBound Publishers, Landover, MD

Within My Window is a collection of "thoughts-full" poetry from an *awakening* moment in my life. This *awakening* was a period of *conscious* spiritual growth that I had not ever experienced. My poetry does not reflect a formal or proper way of writing poetry – it simply reflects "thoughts-full" of feelings placed into a rhythm of words and breaths that attempt to utter my feelings.

The knowledge I gained during this *awakening* was how I really viewed myself – *beneath the surface* – and how important we are to one another. While it's easy to *feel* the importance of loved ones, it's often difficult to discern the importance of others – especially those whom we prefer not to befriend. More importantly, I was *awakened* to the fact that I had a fear of 'failing to match-up to the opinions of others'! (Wow! And I thought I was confident with high self-esteem!) Yet, *out of my slumber and into my awakening* came an immediate acceptance of this: the most important opinion was the *self* opinion - *mine*: How well has *self* progressed through the decades? How well has *self* served others? What is *self's* purpose in life? How effective has *self* used God-given talents? While the opinions of others have a place in our lives, such opinions need to always be in their *proper* place – *behind the opinion of self when the self-opinion speaks the grander truth.*

On the surface, we usually look very good! Yet, when you enter that *private place* – that place that is viewed with the Creator – you discover things that you failed to see on the surface level. In *that place,* you also discover the beauty of your *true self!* It's within your window that you think, say, and feel as you please and at your behest. You get to know and love you – *the real self – so that you can truly get to know and love others. Within My Window* is a peek into my private place that only I (and the Creator) have the freedom to enter without invitation.

Others' opinions (philosophy) are one side to life's story … my opinion is just another side to the *same* story. When we finally learn *to accept both sides* of life's story, we truly begin to accept the way the Creator accepts us – *with love, unconditionally.*

I invite you to take a peek …*Within My Window.*

Table of Contents

1st Peek: Acknowledging The Creator

Reunion

(©2008 Valencia Darnita Robinson)

I re-united with Life recently,

remembering that He Is –

Invincible in His purpose …

Stupendous in His glory …

Patient with His tolerance …

Abundant in His love …

Awesome in His presence.

And, after our reunion,

I *finally* realized that He will never leave me.

The magnificence of the Great I Am cannot

be described with mere words …

All I *know* is that God Is.

Beyond this day,

there is a reason for my presence

which I have yet to understand.

Here, I strive to know why

I am where I am, today,

when I thought I had it all together!

Another test!

Oh, not me again!

You find favor with me day after day,

in spite of my weaknesses and shortcomings.

Another day, another trial, and <u>each time</u>

I claim another victory!

Though I don't always recognize the victory,

especially when the burden seems too hard to carry,

I know that all You do is for my good

and to glorify You!

Well, this day, before the next moment arrives,

I say "thank You" my Exalted Glory,

my Victory, my Joy, my Life ...

for allowing me this one-more-day!

(©1996 Valencia Damita Robinson)

Just As The Flower

The blossoming of a flower indicates only the fruition of its life –
for the true path of the seed's roots is unknown to onlookers.
The graceful wilting of the flower signifies, in turn, the beginning of a new end.

The "new end" is the blossoming of another flower and its predestined wilting.
And, as the "new end" ushers in perhaps the same flower,
each new flower will affirm its own paramount beauty and succumb via its own
predestined end.

Our lives should resemble a flower:
planting of the seeds (children),
developing and strengthening our roots (family),
blossoming (fruitful lives),
and, in time,
gracefully wilting (death).

In planting our seeds, we must properly cultivate the soil
for the roots to develop.
If the roots strengthen and take the right path throughout life,
the fruit of the seed will blossom with unquestionable beauty.

And, after the timely and sufficient display of the blossom's beauty,
the graceful wilting will commence.
Once the blossom has come to its final resting place,
a "new end" will arise
to exude its beauty within a predestined time.

The source of fruitful seeds, strong roots, beautiful blossoms, and graceful wilting
is the same powerful and loving source of our lives …
God.

If God is our primary focus from the planting to the wilting,
then our living has not been in vain.

He is the Glory of it all.

From Now Until Then

From now until then,
I will rise with the sunshine,
shining with the joy that another day will bring.

From now until then,
I will flow with the wind,
blowing the calmness of "inner" peace to all I greet.

From now until then,
I will fall quietly like the rain,
saturating you with My kindness and all the love I have.

From now until then,
I will glow like the moonlight,
glowing over the lives below me with the sureness of My presence.

From now until then,
I will ripple like waves in an ocean,
constantly exploding with high tides of humility, strength and courage.

From now … I will be The Guardian of your precious life … until then.

2nd Peek: About Children

The Blessings of A Child You See ...

The blessings of a child you see
are beyond what we believe them to be ...
We assume that because they are so small
that they lack reality and can't tell it all.
However, as they always show
they know a lot more than we know.
Like how we treat them when we're mad
we get angry at them and make them sad.
Yet, they take the blame, hoping it'll pass
to find us happy again, maybe it'll last.
As a new day comes, they hope for joy
from mom and dad, forget the toy...

They want our love and our affection,
but we seem to focus on imperfection
of their unlearned ways of doing things
like washing their hands or tieing
shoestrings.
We lack the patience and awareness of
their focus
As to how they see things, such as magic –
"hocus pocus."
We want them "little" when all is fine;
yet, we want them "grown" when we're
stressed – so, where's the line?

We say we work to support their needs
like a house, food, clothes – we're just
doing our good deeds.
But we work all day and into the night
to support them in a way we believe right.
And after working and our own social
play,
we simply lack time for them on any given
day.
So, they sit and ponder about what to do
to get mom and dad's attention,
if only we knew ...

They act out their hurt without the notion
that it frustrates us and causes a lot of
commotion.
So, what do you do to ease their pain ...
First, recognize your blessing and you'll
gain ...
insight of how they perceive life –
and all their wonders of it, without the
strife.

The blessings of a child you see
are beyond our own reality ...
They're little today and grown tomorrow,
but if you don't make time for them
it could be your sorrow.
If they don't grow up before your eyes,
God may take them ...
the saddest good-byes.

So, the blessings of a child you see
are here for you to enjoy and be ...
unselfish, patient and tolerant to
the children you have – they're depending
on you ...
to be all that you need to be ...
They're your blessing, can't you see?

What is This Shadow?

(©1997 Valencia Damita Robinson)

What is this shadow that I often see
constantly, *constantly* just staring at me?
Is this shadow just a reflection of my past,
or just a vision of myself in the so-called "looking" glass?

Why is this shadow always, *always* on my mind,
regardless of where I am, and regardless of the time?
How does this shadow always seem to know
every move I make and every place I go?
Who is this shadow that I can't seem to hide,
clinging to me constantly, watching my every stride?

Well, listen carefully, 'cause you need to know:
this constant shadow that I can't seem to let go
is as much a part of me as it is of you –
it's a lost child, and he belongs to you, too!
Just read the newspaper, and you'll see what I mean,
this shadow is a lost boy, pretending to be "Mean Joe Green."

This constant shadow is more than you and I can see,
he's a hurt, hurting child desperately trying to flee …
from his lonely childhood, so unstable and unfair;
to get from each day, he must always take a "dare."

Yet, the constant shadow is not only the boy 'who wish he could' …
but it's also the lonely girl, who's very often misunderstood.
This shadow I see constantly, *constantly* staring at me
is just one of many reflections of the parents we have yet to be ….

You see, these very special shadows that we try to ignore
have us gripping in fear, for we don't know on what day they'll score –
another young death to die by a shadow's young hand …
another funeral possession, more cries, still not many will take a stand.

Not a stand in public for a commitment to fight crime,
but a stand in *our hearts*, to give these lost children some of our time –
To listen to their hearts and offer our love and honest support,
for we were once children and, too, needed strong rapport.

The lives of your very children may be at home and, you *think*, secure,
but keep ignoring the shadow and – bang! – it may be yours!
Taking a moment to show "love" to a child you have not known
might keep the shadow's hand from your child's life … yes, the child of *your* own.

My Beautiful Daughter

The brightest shining star captures the essence of your smile,
my lovely daughter.

The ocean at high tide imitates the energy exuded from your spirit,
my spiritual daughter.

The echo of the sea shell hints to the softness of your voice,
my gentle daughter.

The force of the wind carries the strength of your character,
my courageous daughter.

The beauty of the landscape mirrors your inner beauty,
my humble daughter.

Yet, not a star, an ocean, a shell, the wind, or the landscape
can reflect the love that I have for you – my beautiful daughter.

In My Haste

(©2008 Valencia Damita Robinson)

It's a Boy – A soon-to-be "man-child"!

Handsome – Better looking than most!

Strong – Able to hold his own!

Determined – To get his way at all costs!

Courageous – Not afraid of any thing!

Witty – Keeps us laughing!

Smart – A genius in the making!

Athletic – The best player in the sport!

Successful – A self-made business man!

Look at my "boy-child" and what he's going to be,
I'm growing him up faster than he can understand or see.

In my haste, I've determined the "type" of man he'll grow into –
the macho, hold-those-feelings-back type-of-dude you know …
that has difficulty dealing with his feelings and letting things go.

In my haste, I forget to show him plenty of affection,
thinking since he's a boy, hey, he just needs direction!

Yet, in my haste to make him "the man" I believe he should be …
I do know *he will choose* the type of man we'll later see.

And, in my haste, to rush his childhood that will quickly be gone,
I only pray that my love will keep him steady and strong …

In my haste.

3rd Peek: Parental Favor

Assuredly, My Mother

She heard my cries even though no one else heard me.
~ Yes, but you fulfilled my "cry" first.

She caught me as I fell, when no one else seemed to notice.
~ Of course, your eyes were always on me.

She felt my struggles when no one else seemed to care.
~ You felt mine as I carried you.

She praised my triumphs, though no one else acknowledged them.
~ They were just reflections of my thoughts of you.

She's the best person to ever come into my life.
~ Thank God for the best life that I could have ever had … yours.

To be A Mother to A Daughter ... Such as Me

(©1997 Valencia Darnita Robinson)

To be a mother to a daughter ... such as me,
I know it wasn't always the easiest to be.

Yet, you continued to be "Mom" in spite of all of my tears,
and, without me even knowing it, we cried <u>together</u> for many years.

You were my peace and my security from the very beginning,
laughing and talking with me, I'd often find you just grinning ...

at my girlish ways and then my teenage changes
that kept your head "aching" – I spoke that difficult teenage language!

And, at times, I would mock your peculiar ways of being a mother;
Yet, you still loved me each day, unconditionally – a typical mother.

We've had many good times and, of course, the not-so-good ones, too,
but still no matter what, I've kept on lovin' you.

A mother like you is not that easy to find,
with so much patience and tolerance, you had to have a strong "peace" of mind.

You became a woman-turned-Mom for a daughter ... such as me,
and I "thank you" for your love and the years you've shared with me.

A Father

(©1997 Valencia Darnita Robinson)

A father's presence is like that of an army –
it demands respect.

A father's voice is like that of a prophet –
it commands attention.

A father's spirit resembles that of nature –
it strives to accommodate.

A heart of love belongs to a father.

The Hidden Powers of a Mother's Love

A mother's love is similar to a magician …
able to exude a power that's strong
and confident, yet "mystical" ….

It's a love that's faithful as the sunrise …
always arising and shining with all her "warmth,"
even when hidden by the clouds or threatened by a storm.

A mother's love resembles jewels
secured deep within the ocean …
never knowing what you'll find,
but sure that whatever she commands to the surface
will embrace you with the beauty of her love.

Her love mimics time …
full of expression, enduring, and endless –
forever faithful in never missing a moment.

A mother's love enables you to love.

4th *Peek: For My Hue*

For Sisters Only

My Beautiful Sisters, follow me … to a place in time when we were free
to rule over the Nile and the adjacent land,
while we birthed our children and offered others a strong hand.

My African Sisters, go with me … and explore the truth of our ancient history.
Learn of Queen Nzinga who fought with her might
to keep African people free – that was her plight.

My Spiritual Sisters, fly with me … on a wonderful journey across the sea.
To the Mother Land that once was home,
where we walked as queens and priestesses as we watched the animals roam.

My Gifted Sisters, think with me …
about the talents we're blessed with to use as we
build up our families to make them strong
in the ways that are right – steering them from wrong.

My Powerful Sisters, this is our plight:
to ask God for strength on each day and each night
as we forge our way through the chaotic mess,
back to our rightful places … as Queens and no less.
We must band together to support our Brothers
in their return to their Kingships and due respect from all others.
Our children are our harvests – the special and blessed kind,
so we must carefully guard them from the wrongful of mind.

My Magnificent Sisters, I'm sorry for any ado,
that has brought anything less than sisterhood between me and you.
From this moment forward, I will aspire to be
the most faithful of sisters – you can count on me.
And as we go through each day, we may not always agree,
but with respect and our focus we can stand strongly together
and set our people free …

Oh, Beautiful Black Family

Where can you be?
Your existence must last through eternity …

through the future generations of time
that will hold your rich past …
so full of *courage, strength, humility*
all the Godly things that will last …

from moment to moment and year to year,
never losing *faith* that God is always near.

Oh, Beautiful Black Family what must we do?
We have to keep this family together not just for one or two!
But for all children of today and those of tomorrow
who look trustingly into our eyes, deserving more than sorrow.

So, Beautiful Black Family it's past time to set free
all negative things that harm and stunt the family tree.
Oh, Beautiful Black Family, I know where you must be!
Somewhere lovingly attending the fruit of God's tree.

5th *Peek: On Sorrow*

Joy's Awaiting!
(©1996 Valencia Darnita Robinson)

Each day is the beginning of another end:
the end of yesterday, the end of today, the end
of what will be tomorrow.

Yet, with each end, there's a new beginning:
a beginning to unfold from yesterday, to renew today,
and to begin again tomorrow.

At the beginning of this end, there will be joy ~~
joy to relish in what yesterday tore from your heart ...
the *beauty* of the life lost, in spite of how that life was lost.

There was a right choice in yesterday that could have been made,
but it wasn't ... so, today, you sit and wonder, "why"?
Wonder not, for in yesterday you gave all that God
allowed of your giving ... and none more.
Wonder not about "if things were different today"
because "if" had the opportunity ....

Stay out of tomorrow, for it can burden you
with today's sorrows, just thinking "maybe tomorrow
the hurt will get better."

Today is where you should be,
knowing that the worse has come and gone ...
"inner" peace has arrived, awaiting for you to dismantle sorrow.

The life *departed* is in God's hands now ... and, for you, joy's awaiting.

6th Peek: Be Encouraged

My Simple Old Way

My friends told me the other day
Not to worry, it would be okay.
Yet, my children keep screaming about having their way.
My husband's gone, and didn't say …
where he was going, just gone for the day.
Leaving me, as usual, to find my way.
I gotta raise our children to be okay …
Hoping they'll grow up and be fine some day.

But my friends keep tellin' me, "it'll be okay."
The bills will get paid some kinda way.
The children will grow up and stop the rough play,
and they'll make me proud on one sure day.
So, I just keep on going and often I pray:

"God, please let me have my simple old way …
to pay the bills before the new day,
so the lights can stay on, and we can see our way.
To feed my children each and every day
with only healthy foods, grown with a sun ray.
To clothe my children in an acceptable way
that keeps them from shame on any given day.
To provide a home where they love to stay
that's full of love, mom and dad, and little dismay.

Well, my friends kept tellin' me, "It'll be okay"'
Just be patient and wait, God will see to my way
of providing for our needs, in spite of my dismay.
So, I sat and I waited and heard God say,
"since you've trusted and waited on me each day,
from this point forward, you may have your simple old way."

Unpredictable and mysterious,

running on a continuum between love and hate.

Never knowing which way to turn

from one moment to the next.

Shining brilliantly at the rise of morning,

yet, at times, barely shining by sunset.

Exhausted not from stress of a challenging day,

but exhausted without real explanation.

At times, crushed and with little hope of being repaired.

But as the moon glows brightly,

composure is regained and becoming stronger

with each passing moment.

Often, trusted to others and, unbeknownst to all,

crushed again. This time, a little harder and the pain

last a little longer….

Crushed from love lost, life departed, or trust betrayed.

Still, managing to pull back together,

perhaps now doubting others and questioning sense of worth,

the desire to go on pushes forward 'til at the top again!

Oh, no! Not, again!

Yes, again … and this time hope becomes even dimmer …

But, again, managing to regroup and go forward,

stronger for the next challenge … and it will arrive!

Yet, in spite of all, a *sense of real peace and security* arrives.

Not knowing why so much fluctuation has occurred,

just knowing that it has occurred and it needs to stop!

But it won't … yet, through it all and with more still to come,

a place within you is being prepared by the Spirit of God,

allowing you a "trusting" place where you can finally rest,

your feelings.   (©1996 Valencia Darnita Robinson)

Just Walk Away

(©1997 Valencia Darnita Robinson)

Walk away from choices that often
leave you "stranded" and 'a stray,'
and hold onto choices that encourage your growth
and secure for you a positive and productive day.

Walk away from desires that you know
can only do you some harm,
and hold on to desires that highlight your "inner" beauty,
which far outweighs any false charm.

Walk away from experiences that
have settled in your "closet" for many years,
and know that by forgiving those that harmed you
will loosen their control over you and cease all your tears.

Walk away from insecurities and jealousies alike
and begin to renew 'within,'
allowing your goodness and beauty to flow
that you've kept hidden from 'way-back-you-know-when.'

Walk away from people who insist that their negative ways
are okay and *all about them* is just fine,
and recognize and accept that, if people do change,
it will be at their will … disconnect the phone or just hang up the line!

Just walk away from your weaknesses and others' opinions
of you that really don't equal a dime,
and walk straight into the strength of your character, as it should be –
stop wasting this life – it's your one and only time!

Just walk away …

7th Peek: The Inner Being

This Blossom

There is a blossom within me that seeks to grow,
but I hinder its growth with my doubts,
my fears,
my insecurities,
my jealousies,
and all my selfish ways.

Yet, this blossom no matter how many times I thwart its growth,
pushes forward – any way –
in spite of my shortcomings.
Trying and testing me each step of its growing way,
urging me on in ways I have yet to understand!
It fights me daily to strip me of my misplaced pride,
teaching me to humble myself.

Though I moan and groan and cry 'til I can't cry – No More –
this blossom just won't stop!
Still, urging me into areas of my life … that life within me … that fear
has kept me away from for so, so long.
Forcing me to look deeper, search harder for the answer!
But look at what? Search where?
Answer me? Why can't You just answer me?

All of my life, without even knowing, this same blossom
has diligently grown inside me to give me Life's most precious treasure …

The blossom that grows diligently and faithfully within me is "inner peace."
Although I still thwart its growth, I know that It's patience with me
will allow this blossom to one day come to fruition.

And "inner peace" will be mine to relish in its beauty.

It's invisible and often times
creeps upon us
when we least expect it.
It's around daily,
no matter what we do
or how we think.
It's constantly stagnating
our minds,
making us believe things
that could not possibly be true!
It watches our every move,
hoping to catch us off guard.
It's always looking
for ways to thwart our every step,
to hinder our growth,
to keep us always facing backwards!
We strive boldly and earnestly
to conquer it!
We fight with all
our might to defeat it daily.
Still, no matter how hard we try,
no matter what we do,
no matter what we think or what we say,
it finds its way back
into our lives …
again, yearning to
keep us from being
who we're destined to be!
Yet, in spite of its
persistence, it can't
get a firm grip on us!
We fight it with all
our might and, though
we don't always win
each battle, the battles
we win far outweigh
the losses suffered!
It's an enemy to be
fought to its death!
An enemy that will lose
as long as we stay focused!
With the Spirit guiding us,
this enemy can never claim us!
Fear.

Just Imagine

Just imagine if tomorrow
brought you everything,
but took away the songs that birds sing.

Just imagine if yesterday
would come again,
but in return took everything of today that you worked so hard to win.

Or, if today
would last forever and a year,
but took from your heart all memories of past joy that you long to keep near.

Just imagine how life
might be,
if you were granted a wish on everything that you desire to see ...

And on that wish,
you wished away the pain and sorrow,
but without the suffering how would you really grow and improve for a better tomorrow?

Or for that wish,
you wished that all things would go your way,
but truly how many people would be willing to agree to all the things you say?

Just imagine,
if you were a better person than you often pretend to be,
there would be no need for fantasy wishes and all the things you desire to see ...

Because your inner being
would reflect the beauty of your soul
and life, as it is, would be a wonderful place to behold.

Just imagine,
how beautiful the world would be
if we all took the time to set the ugliness within our souls free ...

Imagine,
all the great things you can do,
by diligently working inwardly to become a more beautiful you.

Just imagine ...

It's as gentle as a summer breeze,

yet it fills you with the strength of a lion.

Its pending arrival is never announced,

but you know when it's present.

It engulfs you in its mystical powers;

however, you can't tell for how long it will stay.

It overwhelms you with its calmness,

and you're amazed at its ability to relax you.

You seek its presence daily;

however, it seems to come only when you most need it.

You strive to hold onto the calm that it brings into your life;

however, you find that your calm is only temporary.

You, therefore, work desperately to keep the "calm,"

but, in turn, release it and the storm reappears.

And, after the storm reappears,

your life returns to its former state.

Now, you must begin again the cycle

of working to regain the "calm" …

Except, next time, you'll be able to relish a

bit longer in your long-awaited and seemingly overdue

breath of fresh air!

Today, I found out something new about myself ...
something that I struggled with for many years.

And, *oh*, what a wonderful feeling!

Today, I learned that I can forgive – truly forgive and mean it!
No more smiling on the outside, while all along still angry and hurt on the
inside.

Oh, what a wonderful feeling!

Today, I took the first step ... a real step forward
to put the past behind me.
To move forward this day, only looking back as a reminder
of the lesson learned.

Though, today, I still struggle with other "yesterdays"
that must be put behind me ...
At least, now, I have one less "yesterday" to deal with ...
and better able to deal with just *today*.

If tomorrow is allowed,
then I'll have another day to put behind "yesterday,"
and look forward to enjoying just today!

Oh, what a wonderful feeling!

8th Peek: Well!

Excuse Me

Excuse me for knowing a little less than you do,
especially when it concerns things particular to you.

Excuse me for being a bit too polite today,
but being so is the only "polite" way …
to handle your ignorance in the things you believe I should know;
yet, you haven't given me any insight or even time to grow
and learn of the knowledge you hide within your mind,
this very knowledge you seem to believe that we share in-kind.

Excuse me for not catering to your desires and your needs,
but, in my mind, it's God first so the heck with your deeds ….

Until I am all that God will have me to be,
you'll just have to settle for what you simply desire to see …
and if what you see is just not good enough
I suggest you get over it, because I intend to be and do what I must ….

Excuse me for ignoring the limits of your narrow mind,
for you'll NEVER hold captive the strength of my spirit – not now or any time.

The beauty and strength of Spirit that I possess is not for me alone,
you have it, too; just listen to the Spirit or simply reap the seeds you have sown.
If I don't act in the ways that you perceive to be "right,"
it's because I seek to do God's will – not to be pleasing within your sight!

So, if you'll excuse me for not acting in the way you desire when we greet,
I'll have reason to excuse the "less than" of you when we next meet.

9th Peek: Friendship

Friendships blossom like a flower …
never knowing quite when they'll bloom,
only sure that they'll be beautiful.

And as soon as blossoms reach their "peak" of beauty,
they wither quicker than they grew.
And like a blossom, our friendship reached its peak –
so full of joy and trust and a comfort to behold.

Yet, unlike the blossom, the "withering" is a
much longer process …
for our withering involves distance –
the "distancing" of our long conversations, our laughs,
and our crying together.

Our "distance" appears from our differences and
our opinions of the other.
And with "distance," space and time evolves –
increasing the space between us and the time spent together,
testing the strength of our friendship.

But, like the blossom that returns year after year,
stronger, healthier, and more beautiful …
so returns our friendship,

striving to remove the obstacles mixed
within our "souls," ensuring our friendship's blossoming.

At times, we may feel the strength of a storm uprooting us,
taking the joy we once shared.
Yet, like the sunshine that hides high above
the clouds and beyond the haze …
the storm passes, the sun shines,
and our friendship, again,
withstands the elements.

So, as the seasons pass and the storm
threatens the blossom's return,
so will our friendship …
pass from one year to the next,

claiming what the storm dare not take –
our joy, our strength, and our friendship.
(©1997 Valencia Darnita Robinson)

Final Peek: Nothing Like It ... Love

My Shoreline and Your Tide

(©1997 Valencia Darnita Robinson)

Love, like the wind, never warns you
from which direction it's coming.
Before you know it, it has you in a whirlwind
and you don't know which direction to move.

Love, like the ocean, is ceaseless:
constantly moving and wavering in unpredictable waves.
Yet, like a tide resting on the shoreline,
you know that true love will always return.

Like a ship in the ocean so strong and so mighty,
love is steady and strong enough to ride the tide …
for within my ocean of love, I found a treasure:
a beautiful jewel that I had not searched, but happily fell upon.

This jewel of love I found is like the ocean,
at times, unpredictable, yet confidently rests
each day on the shoreline of my heart.

This jewel of love is also like the wind,
blowing strongly in my direction,
yet gently, allowing me to freely flow toward it.

For you are the jewel that God has placed in my heart,
resting confidently at my shoreline and allowing
my love to flow freely toward you.

And in the whirlwind of your life you shall find my love: blowing constantly,
yet gently, but blowing with all my might …
to love you in all the ways that I am capable,
in every way which God has deemed right.

For you, my love, are my shoreline and I am the tide,
confidently returning to you each day.

This Time

(©1997 Valencia Darnita Robinson)

This time, I will listen with my heart,
feeling all that you have to give me.
Knowing that with each beat,
a new surge of love will vibrantly
whisk my way! Carrying me
to a deeper depth of your love.

> *This time, I'll listen with my eyes,*
> *observing all that you say and do.*
> Noticing the way you move your
> lips and how often you blink your eyes.
> Watching as your brows raise and when
> they relax ... allowing your eyes to
> captivate and hold me.

> *This time, I'll listen with my ears,*
> *hearing every word you say.*
> Engulfing all that is good that flows
> from your lips, and quickly disposing
> that which stands to harm us. Knowing,
> that as you speak, whispers of your love
> flow gently toward me.

> *This time, I'll feel you with my emotions,*
> *caressing your kindness and gentleness.*
> Noting the effects of our moods,
> feeling your joy and sadness and knowing
> that you, too, are feeling mine.

> *This time, I'll love you as the sun rises,*
> *arising early to bask in all of your beauty.*
> Endeavoring to feel your love at your
> highest peak and seeking to secure it
> before it settles.

> *This time, I'll take my time and hold onto our joy,*
> *while loving you as you desire ... this time.*

www.ingramcontent.com/pod-product-compliance
Lightning Source LLC
Chambersburg PA
CBHW032036090426
42741CB00006B/837